THE ULTIMATE

Cartoonist and comedy writer John Byrne is a joke expert, who has published many best-selling joke books. He lives in London with his wife and family. They are the first people he tries his jokes

Some other fun-filled books by John Byrne

MAD MAGS: WOOF!
MAD MAGS: PURR!

THE ULTIMATE JOKE HANDBOOK

JOHN BYRNE

PUFFIN BOOKS

For Michael Emmanus

PUFFIN BOOKS

Published by the Penguin Group
Penguin Books Ltd, 27 Wrights Lane, London W8 5TZ, England
Penguin Putnam Inc., 375 Hudson Street, New York, New York 10014, USA
Penguin Books Australia Ltd, Ringwood, Victoria, Australia
Penguin Books Canada Ltd, 10 Alcorn Avenue, Toronto, Ontario, Canada M4V 3B2
Penguin Books (NZ) Ltd, Private Bag 102902, NSMC, Auckland, New Zealand

On the World Wide Web at: www.penguin.com

Penguin Books Ltd, Registered Offices: Harmondsworth, Middlesex, England

First published 1999
1 3 5 7 9 10 8 6 4 2

Copyright © John Byrne, 1999
All rights reserved

The moral right of the author/illustrator has been asserted

Set in Gill Sans

Made and printed in England by Clays Ltd, St Ives plc

British Library Cataloguing in Publication Data
A CIP catalogue record for this book is available from the British Library

ISBN 0–141–30409–X

CONTENTS

A FUNNY THING HAPPENED TO ME ON THE WAY TO YOUR PLANET...

Actually, lots of funny things have happened to me. I'm Woody Alien, by the way, the cosmic comedian from Planet X. At least, I *used* to be from Planet X. But for some reason the other aliens on my planet suggested I go and find some new jokes ...

I can't see why myself, even with my three eyes. I mean, 'Why did the xyrazmzzllmf cross the frodenymyxxl? To get to the bbnnvxfghsywwxl!' What joke could be more hilarious than that?

So I decided to see what you jokesters on Planet Earth could come up with. After all, you lot must have a sense of humour, considering how funny you all look. So here are all the Earthling jokes I've collected — old ones, new ones, jokes on any subject under the sun (and since we have fifteen suns on my planet, that's a lot of jokes).

Not only that, but I'll be popping up throughout the book with some Ultimate Joke Telling Tips to help you take over the universe ... or at least take over the playground with a comedy act that's just out of this world!

ELEPHANT-ASTIC!

THE OLD JOKES ARE ALWAYS THE BEST, SO THEY SAY — AND THESE ARE THE GREYEST AND WRINKLIEST OF THEM ALL!

Why are elephants big and grey and wrinkly?
Because if they were small and white and round, they'd be peppermints.

Why do elephants have trunks?
Because they'd look silly in Y-fronts.

Why do elephants have wrinkles?
Have you ever tried to iron one?

What's grey and wrinkly and goes up and down?
An elephant with hiccups.

What time is
it when the
elephant sits
on the fence?
Time to get a
new fence.

What should you do if
you find an elephant in
your bed?
Sleep somewhere else.

HEY WOODY—
HOW MANY ELEPHANTS
CAN YOU FIT IN
A SPACESHIP?

I DON'T ¿GASP¿
KNOW... I JUST WISH
I'D GOT OUT OF THE
SPACESHIP BEFORE
ANY ELEPHANTS
GOT IN!

What's big, grey and
dangerous?
An elephant with a
machine gun.

Why did the elephant
paint himself yellow?
So he could hide in a bowl
of custard.
Don't be silly – I've never
seen an elephant in a
bowl of custard.
See? It works.

What's grey
and has four
legs and a
trunk?
A mouse going
on holiday.

What's grey and wrinkly and flies?
An elephant in a helicopter.

WAIT! STOP THE ELE-COPTER... I FORGOT TO PACK MY TRUNK!!

Why do elephants have big ears?
Because Noddy won't pay the ransom.

What's big, grey and has sixteen feet?
Four elephants.

Where can you buy cheap elephants?
At a jumbo sale.

What do you give a nervous elephant?
Trunkquillizers.

What's big and grey and wears
rubber boots?
A wellyphant.

What's big, grey
and wrinkly and
never takes a bath?
A smellyphant.

What's big and grey,
plays the piano and
sings?
Ele–ton John.

What's the most
nervous animal in
the jungle?
A yellowphant.

What happens
when elephants
get drunk?
They start seeing
pink people.

I DON'T KNOW ABOUT
YOU LOT, BUT I DON'T
FIND THE JOKES ON THIS
PAGE VERY
ELE-VATING!

GLUMBO

How do you get four elephants into a Mini? Two in the back and two in the front.

IMAGINE A BIG ELEPHANT BEING SCARED OF A LITTLE MOUSE..

HE'S NOT—HE'S SCARED YOU MIGHT TELL HIM A JOKE FROM THIS BOOK!

How do you get four giraffes into a Mini? You can't – it's already full of elephants.

I HEAR YOU KNOW A GREAT JOKE ABOUT ELEPHANT MEMORIES?

How can you tell if an elephant's been in the fridge? Footprints in the butter.

What do elephants do at the end of a long, hard day?
Flop down in front of the ele-vision.

Why did the police arrest the four elephants in their Mini?
For trunk driving.

What do you call a depressed elephant?
Glumbo.

How do you wrap up an elephant?
With a big roll of ele-tape.

I USED TO... BUT I'VE FORGOTTEN IT!

How do elephants
climb stairs?
They don't – they use
the ele-vator.

How do
elephants travel?
By Jumbo Jet.

Ultimate Joke Telling Tip 1

Make sure that you practise telling your jokes before trying them out on your friends. Getting the words wrong can really ruin your punchlines!

MY FEET ARE KILLING ME! HOW MANY TIMES DO I NEED TO WALK ACROSS THE ROAD 'TIL YOU GET IT RIGHT?

WHAT CAN I DO? SURELY YOU DON'T WANT ME TO GET TOO COCKY?

CHICKEN CHUCKLES

HERE ARE SOME
'HEN-SATIONAL'
EARTHLING
FAVOURITES WITH
A FEW 'EGG-STRA'
SPECIAL JOKES
THROWN IN!

Why did the chicken cross the road?
For its own foul reasons.

Why did the chicken cross the road?
To get to the other side.

YECCH!
IF YOU'RE
LOOKING
FOR GOOD
JOKES,
YOU'RE
OUT OF
CLUCK!

RUN!! WE'VE GOT TO HATCH A SCHEME TO ESCAPE FROM THAT UNFUNNY ALIEN!

YOU'RE RIGHT— I'VE HEARD MORE THAN ENOUGH OF HIS CRACKS!

Why did the chicken cross the road?
It was looking for a bit of egg-citement.

**Why did the chicken cross the road?
Because if it had tried to cross the motorway, it would have been flattened.**

Why did the duck cross the road?
Because it was glued to the chicken.

Why did the chicken cross the road?
Because all the other crossings were for zebras.

**Why did the chicken cross the road?
For its own hentertainment.**

Why did the caterpillar cross the road?
Because it loved doing impersonations of chickens.

Why did the chicken cross the road?
I don't know – it was on the other side before I got the chance to ask it.

Why did the lorry cross the road the wrong way?
It was swerving to avoid the chicken.

Why did the chicken cross the road?
It was on the way to a cock-a-doodle-do.

COME BACK! DON'T YOU WANT TO HEAR ANY MORE OF MY GREAT CHICKEN JOKES?

NO THANKS... I'M MAKING A DASH FOR THE EGGS-IT!

11

HAVE YOU HEARD ...?

ASK A STUPID QUESTION, GET A STUPID ANSWER— IT'S THE SAME WHICHEVER PLANET YOU COME FROM!

Have you heard the one about the messy bed?
No, it hasn't been made up yet.

Have you heard the one about the three eggs?
No? Two bad.

Have you heard the one about the three holes in the ground?
No? Well, well, well.

Have you heard the one about the embarrassed sheep?
No? Shame on ewe.

THAT ALIEN'S HOLE JOKES ARE REALLY THE PITS!

Have you heard the one about the butter?
Yes, but don't spread it about.

Have you heard the one about the head?
Yes, but I'm keeping it under my hat.

Have you heard the one about the two haddock?
Yes, but it sounds a bit fishy.

Have you heard the one about the very old cartwheel?
Yes, it's been going around for years.

Have you heard the one about the very small earthquake?
Yes, but it was no great shakes.

Hi! HAVE YOU HEARD THE ONE ABOUT THE ALIEN WHO KNOWS LOTS OF JOKES?

NO... AND IF I CAN PUT SOME SPACE BETWEEN US, I WON'T HAVE TO!

Have you heard the one about the two polar bears and a penguin?
Yes, but it's snow joke.

Have you heard the one about the cement?
Yes, but I've got it a bit mixed up.

Have you heard the one about the porcupine?
Yes, but I couldn't quite grasp it.

Have you heard the one about the Polo Mint?
Yes, it's on the tip of my tongue.

Have you heard the one about the punching bag?
Yes, it really knocked me out.

Have you heard the one about the sore throat?
Yes, it left me speechless.

Have you heard the one about the electricity bill?
Yes, I got a real shock.

Have you heard the one about the skunk?
Yes, it really stinks.

Have you heard the one about the broken picture frame?
Yes, but I couldn't get the hang of it.

Have you heard the joke that goes 'ha, ha, ha'?
Yes, it's a real laugh.

Ultimate Joke Telling Tip 2

Don't start telling another joke until everyone has finished laughing at the one before – otherwise they won't hear what you're talking about.

HYENA CAGE

HA HA HA HA HA HA HA HA HA HA HA

I'M REALLY GLAD YOU LIKED THE JOKE I TOLD YOU... BUT THAT WAS TWO HOURS AGO...

I SAY, I SAY, I SAY

THESE JOKES CERTAINLY LEFT ME SPEECHLESS!

What did one wall say to the other wall?
'Meet you at the corner.'

What did one sheep say to the other sheep?
'See ewe later.'

WOODY THINKS HE'S A COMEDIAN—BUT HE CAN'T PULL THE WOOL OVER MY EYES!

What did one eye say to the other eye? 'Something's come between us and it smells.'

THIS JOKE REALLY GETS UP MY NOSE!

What did the nose say to the eyes? 'You two are always looking down on me.'

WHAT DID ONE KANGAROO SAY TO THE OTHER KANGAROO?

HERE COMES WOODY ALIEN... LET'S HOP IT!

What did the python say to the explorer? 'I've got a crush on you.'

What did the candle say to the matchstick? 'You're starting to get on my wick.'

What did one banana say to the other banana? 'Let's split ... unless you're too yellow.'

What did one watch say to the other watch?
'You and I could have a good time together.'

I LIKE THESE - JOKES!

What did the doctor say to the big vitamin pill?
'I'm finding you very hard to take.'

What did one rooster say to the other rooster?
'How do you cock-a-doodle-doo?'

YES, BUT YOU'RE CUCKOO!

What did the old fishmonger say to the young fishmonger?
'It's time you knew your plaice.'

What did one king say to the other king?
'Looks like reign again.'

18

What did one witch say to other witch?
'Let's pop outside for a spell...'

EYE OF NEWT, EAR OF BAT, WOODY'S JOKES ARE PRETTY FLAT!

What did Batman's mum say to him at five o'clock?
'Come and get your dinner, dinner, dinner...'

What did the cat say to the mouse?
'Catch you later.'

What did one fire say to the other fire?
'Let's go out together.'

WHAT DID THE REALLY FUNNY COMEDIAN SAY TO THE AUDIENCE?

NOTHING! WE WERE GONE BEFORE HE GOT THE CHANCE!

What did one raspberry say to the other raspberry? 'How did we get into this jam?'

What did one vampire say to the other vampire? 'Fangs ain't what they used to be.'

EEK! TO LIKE THESE JOKES YOU'D **HAVE** TO BE BATTY!

Ultimate Joke Telling Tip 3

Let some of your friends get a joke in edgeways every so often – you want to be a comedian not just a big show off!

SEE? I TOLD YOU HE HAD SO MANY JOKES THAT WE SHOULD TAPE THEM!

=MMMPH!=

EXTRA STICKY

MUMMY MADNESS

UNLIKE EARTHLING MUMS AND DADS, PARENTS FROM MY PLANET ARE VERY GOOD LISTENERS – PROBABLY BECAUSE THEY'VE EACH GOT SEVEN EARS!

'Mummy, Mummy, can I go skateboarding?'
'Fine, but if you break both your legs, don't come running to me.'

'Mummy, Mummy, I've hurt my leg – what should I do?'
'Limp!'

WOODY OFFERED TO WRITE A JOKE ON MY PLASTER CAST – I FEEL LIKE RUNNING ALREADY!

MUM SAYS IF I'M NAUGHTY SHE WON'T LET WOODY ALIEN TELL ME ONE OF HIS JOKES...

MY MUM SAYS IF I'M GOOD SHE WON'T LET WOODY TELL ME ANY OF HIS JOKES!

'Mummy, Mummy, all the other kids call me a werewolf.'
'Just ignore them, dear – now wipe your eyes and go and comb your face.'

'Mummy, Mummy, can I play with Grandpa?'
'No – I've told you not to keep digging him up!'

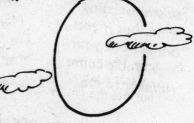

I'M NOT HOWLING BECAUSE THERE'S A FULL MOON – I'VE SEEN WOODY'S ACT!

'Mummy, Mummy, why are your hands so soft?'
'Shut up and wash the dishes!'

'Mummy, Mummy, why are you angry? I've spent the whole day sitting here reading.'
'Yes, but the rest of us would like to use the toilet too.'

'Mummy, Mummy, when I grow up I want to drive a steamroller.'
'Well, I won't stand in your way.'

'Mummy, Mummy, I get a pain in my eye every time I drink my tea.'
'Try taking the spoon out first.'

'Mummy, Mummy, I fed the goldfish.'
'Yes, but I didn't mean feed him to the cat.'

'Mummy, Mummy, you said I could throw rice at my sister's wedding.'
'Yes, but not the kind you get in tins.'

IF I DON'T GET OUT OF THIS BOOK SOON, THERE'LL BE TROUBLE BREWING!

WHAT AN INSULT!

IT'S BEST NOT TO USE ANY OF THESE INSULTS, UNLESS YOU WANT PEOPLE TO THINK YOU'RE A LITTLE MONSTER. OF COURSE ON MY PLANET WE USE THEM ALL THE TIME BECAUSE WE <u>ARE</u> LITTLE MONSTERS!

'I'd like to say you're a wonderful singer – so it's a real pity you're not.'

'I can tell you have a bath regularly – it must be at least once a year.'

'When you go to the zoo, you need two tickets – one to get in and one to get out.'

'You're a real treasure – everyone wants to know where you were dug up.'

'You deserve a little respect – as little as possible.'

'You're good for my health – every time I see you, I feel like taking a long walk.'

'You're lucky – if you went out of your mind, no one would notice the difference.'

'When you grow up you should be an optician – you're always making a spectacle of yourself.'

'You should buy a dress to match the colour of your eyes – if you can find a bloodshot dress.'

'You can brighten up a room – just by leaving it.'

'Your teeth are like stars – they come out at night.'

'You should be on TV – then we could switch you off.'

Ultimate Joke Telling Tip 4

Never tell the same joke twice to the same audience – no matter how funny it is the first time. Most jokes rely on surprise to make them work.

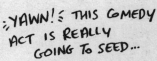

SQUAWK! DID YOU HEAR ABOUT THE PARROT WHO TOLD THE SAME JOKE OVER AND OVER AGAIN?

YAWN! THIS COMEDY ACT IS REALLY GOING TO SEED...

SPORTING SILLINESS

HMMM – I CAN'T QUITE GET MY HEAD AROUND THESE STRANGE EARTH SPORTS. THE ONLY SPORT I KNOW IS PLANET HOPPING!

Why was the football pitch under water?
The players couldn't stop dribbling.

Why do golfers always wear an extra pair of socks?
In case they get a hole in one.

KNOW ANY GOLF JOKES?

TEE HEE.

IF WOODY'S JOKES DON'T IMPROVE HE'S BOUND TO GET THE BOOT!

Who was the world's fastest runner?
Adam, because he came first in the human race.

Why did the coach put sawdust on the rugby pitch?
To stop his team slipping out of the league.

Why is basketball the most respectable sport?
Because everyone looks up to the players.

WOW! YOU'VE BROKEN THE WORLD LAND SPEED RECORD... IS THAT THROUGH YEARS OF HARD WORK AND TRAINING?

NO! IT'S BECAUSE WOODY ALIEN THREATENED TO TELL ME ANOTHER ONE OF HIS AWFUL JOKES!!

The school football coach says there are only two things keeping me out of the first team — my left foot and my right foot.

FIRST GIRL: I've got a couple of medals for running.
SECOND GIRL: I know — you grabbed them and ran out of the trophy room before anyone could catch you!

My uncle put a fiver on a horse in the Grand National. Unfortunately it fell off as soon as the horse started running.

OFF!!

LOOKS LIKE MY COLOURFUL CAREER AS A COMEDIAN IS CONTINUING... MY SPORTS JOKES HAVE GOT ME THE RED CARD!

IT'S A KNOCK OUT!

I NEVER TOUCHED HIM! HE JUST HEARD WOODY'S ACT AND FELL ASLEEP!

BOXER: Have I done the other guy any damage yet?
COACH: No, but keep swinging – the draught might give him a cold.

My little brother was banned from our local leisure centre for weeing in the swimming pool. I told them lots of little boys wee in the swimming pool. They said, 'Yes, but not from the high diving board.'

FIRST BOY: I've been chosen to represent our school in an athletics competition.
SECOND BOY: Who told you that?
FIRST BOY: The Head – he said I was for the high jump.

NAUGHTY NICKNAMES

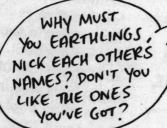

WHY MUST YOU EARTHLINGS, NICK EACH OTHERS NAMES? DON'T YOU LIKE THE ONES YOU'VE GOT?

Our school goalkeeper's called 'Cinderella', because he never gets to the ball.

My little brother's called 'Flannel', because he always shrinks from washing.

All my teachers call me 'Surrender', because they take one look at me and give up.

Our headteacher's called 'Laryngitis', because he's such a pain in the neck.

My sister's nickname is 'Dandruff', because she's a little bit flaky and always getting in your hair.

Our dog is called 'Blacksmith', because every time someone comes into the house he makes a bolt for the door.

ASK A SILLY QUESTION ...

I ASKED ALL MY CLEVEREST ALIEN FRIENDS THESE QUESTIONS... AND THEY DIDN'T KNOW THE ANSWERS EITHER!

Do chickens ever get people pox?

If tin whistles are made out of tin, what do they make fog horns out of?

Can a frog get a person in its throat?

If a fly didn't have any wings would it be called a walk?

Do twins born in Holland speak double Dutch?

If eight out of ten people in this country write with a biro, what do the other two do with it?

If a glass-blower inhales, does he get a pane in his stomach?

If you fall into a barrel of lemons, will you come to a bitter end?

KNOCK, KNOCK!

THESE TERRIBLE JOKES NEED NO INTRODUCTION- THEY'RE BOUND TO KNOCK YOU OUT!

Knock, knock.
Who's there?
Muppet.
Muppet who?
Muppet seven every morning.

Knock, knock.
Who's there?
Roland.
Roland who?
Roland butter's
very tasty.

KNOW WHAT THE KEY TO GOOD HUMOUR IS? LOCKING WOODY OUT AS SOON AS YOU CAN!

Knock, knock.
Who's there?
Ray.
Ray who?
Raydio One's really
boring.

Knock, knock.
Who's there?
Yvonne.
Yvonne who?
Yvonne you to
open the door as
soon as possible.

Knock, knock.
Who's there?
Alex.
Alex who?
Alex plain as soon
as you let me in.

Knock, knock.
Who's there?
Amos.
Amos who?
Amos leave again
soon, so hurry up
and open the door.

Knock, knock.
Who's there?
Wanda.
Wanda who?
Wanda buy a
new stereo?

KNOCK KNOCK!!

ER... WHO'S THERE?

NEVER MIND... IF IT'S THAT AWFUL ALIEN, LOCK HIM OUT!!

Knock, knock.
Who's there?
Isabel.
Isabel who?
Isabel necessary on a bicycle?

THESE ARE WHAT I CALL BAD JOKES WITH KNOBS ON!

Knock, knock.
Who's there?
Hugo.
Hugo who?
Hugoing to let me in or not?

Knock, knock.
Who's there?
Olive.
Olive who?
Olive in this house – what are you doing here?

Knock, knock.
Who's there?
Ivor.
Ivor who?
Ivor you let me or I'll kick the door down.

HELP! I'M STUCK!

TSK, TSK – NO NEED TO GET IN A FLAP!

Knock, knock.
Who's there?
Tick.
Tick who?
Tick 'em up – thith
ith a hold-up!

Knock, knock.
Who's there?
Earl.
Earl who?
Earl catch my death
out here if you
don't let me in.

Knock, knock.
Who's there?
Ivor.
Ivor ready let you in.
I know – Ivor
terrible memory.

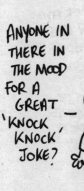

Knock, knock.
Who's there?
Jerry.
Jerry who?
Jerry member to leave the key under the mat like I told you?

Knock, knock.
Who's there?
Trish.
Trish who?
God bless you!

IT'S A NEW MAT FOR WOODY ALIEN!

NOT WELCOME

Knock, knock.
Who's there?
May.
May who?
Maybe I don't want to tell you.

Knock, knock.
Who's there?
Cereal.
Cereal who?
Cereal pain having to stand out here like this.

Knock, knock.
Who's there?
Una.
Una who?
No, I don't – open the door so I can see.

I MAY BE JUST A KEYHOLE BUT MY JOKES ARE A 'HOLE' LOT BETTER THAN THESE!

Knock, knock.
Who's there?
Boo.
Boo who?
No need to cry – it's only a 'Knock, knock' joke.

Knock, knock.
Who's there?
Felix.
Felix who?
Felix tremely impatient – open the door!

Knock, knock.
Who's there?
Nun.
Nun who?
Nun of your business.

KNOCK KNOCK!

WHAT ARE YOU KNOCKING FOR? YOU'RE ALREADY INSIDE..

YES, BUT SO IS WOODY ALIEN... SO NOW I WANT TO GET OUT!!

39

Knock, knock.
Who's there?
Oliver.
Oliver who?
Oliver thing or two to say to you if you don't open the door.

Knock, knock.
Who's there?
Wayne.
Wayne who?
'Wayne a manger, no crib for a bed.'

Knock, knock.
Who's there?
Freeze.
Freeze who?
'Freeze a jolly good fellow.'

IF THESE DOOR JOKES DON'T END SOON, IT'LL BE CURTAINS FOR ME!

Knock, knock.
Who's there?
Emma.
Emma who?
Emma new neighbour and I just called round to introduce myself.

Knock, knock.
Who's there?
Orange.
Orange who?
Orange you glad there are no more 'Knock, knock' jokes?

Knock, knock.
Who's there?
A little man who can't reach the doorbell.

Ultimate Joke Telling Tip 5

Make sure your audience will understand your joke. For instance, if you're telling a joke about Joe Bloggs the famous footballer, begin by saying 'That reminds me of a story about Joe Bloggs – you all know who he is, don't you?' If they don't, remind them before you start telling the joke.

WHY DO MARTIANS HAVE RED SPOTS? BECAUSE PLUTONIANS HAVE PURPLE TOENAILS!

I'M SURE THAT'S REALLY FUNNY...

...IF YOU COME FROM MARS.

WHODUNNIT?

THERE'S NO MYSTERY ABOUT THE FAMOUS NAMES BEHIND THESE INVENTIONS!

Who invented the anorak?
Robin Hood.

Who invented air freshener?
Alexander Graham Smell.

Who invented the fireplace?
Alexander the Grate.

MY QUESTION IS WHO TALKED ME INTO READING THESE AWFUL RIDDLES?

Who invented the five-day week?
Robinson Crusoe – he had all his work done by Friday.

Who invented the wheel?
I don't know, but it certainly caused a revolution.

IT'S NO WONDER WE'RE IN WOODY'S BOOK – THERE'S ALWAYS BEEN A QUESTION MARK OVER HIS COMEDY SKILLS!

Who invented the Time Machine? H. G. Wells – but that won't be until next week.

Who invented fire? Some bright spark.

Who invented acne? Mary Queen of Spots.

Who invented fractions? Henry the Fifth.

WE RECKON WOODY ALIEN INVENTED TIME TRAVEL..

YEAH... WHENEVER HE TELLS ONE OF HIS JOKES IT'S *TIME* YOU WERE TRAVELLING!!

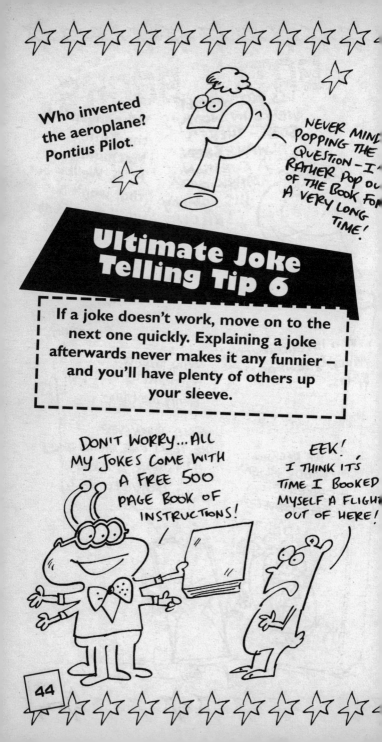

Who invented the aeroplane? Pontius Pilot.

NEVER MIND POPPING THE QUESTION - I RATHER POP OUT OF THE BOOK FOR A VERY LONG TIME!

Ultimate Joke Telling Tip 6

If a joke doesn't work, move on to the next one quickly. Explaining a joke afterwards never makes it any funnier – and you'll have plenty of others up your sleeve.

DON'T WORRY... ALL MY JOKES COME WITH A FREE 500 PAGE BOOK OF INSTRUCTIONS!

EEK! I THINK IT'S TIME I BOOKED MYSELF A FLIGHT OUT OF HERE!

BATTY BOOKS

THESE LITERARY LUNATICS WILL HAVE YOU LAUGHING 'WRITE' AWAY!

TALL STORIES BY G. RAFF

THE SWISS ARMY KNIFE by ANDY DEVICE

RETURN TO JURASSIC PARK by Diana Saur

HAVE YOU READ "A BRICK WALL"?

I FOUND IT VERY HARD TO GET THROUGH!

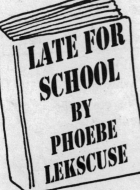

TICKLISH TIPS

You should always listen to good advice – so it's probably best to ignore these tips!

What should you do if you swallow an alarm clock?
Do your best to pass the time.

Why should you never whisper in front of a cornfield?
Because it's all ears.

Where should you take a sick ship?
To the doc.

Why should you never eat an unplucked turkey?
Because it'll make you feel a little down in the mouth.

What should you do if lightning strikes your lavatory?
Don't panic – it's just a flash in the pan.

What should you do if an angry bull's about to charge?
Take away his credit cards.

Why should you never get a job as an archaeologist?
Because your career will be in ruins.

I SAY, I SAY... WHAT'S THE BEST WAY TO TELL A REALLY FUNNY JOKE?

LISTEN TO ONE OF YOURS AND THEN DO EXACTLY THE OPPOSITE!

What should you wear if your donkey has BO?
An ass mask.

What sport should you take up if you're going bald?
Jogging – because you'll soon get some fresh 'air.

WHATCHA-MACALLITS

THESE NONSENSICAL NAMES WILL MAKE YOU SCREAM— FOR HELP!

What do you call someone with sausages in their hair?
A Head Banger.

What do you call someone who peers through a butcher's window?
A Mince Spy.

What do you call a camel with three humps?
Humphrey.

WHAT DO YOU CALL A HYENA IN WOODY'S BOOK?

"A HYENA TRYING TO GET OUT OF WOODY'S BOOK!"

What do you call an insect with a machine gun?
Baddy Long Legs.

What do you call a fly that lives in Russia?
A Moscow-ito.

What do you call two parallel lines of vegetables?
A Dual Cabbageway.

What do you call an elf that eats too fast?
A Goblin.

What do you call a jelly in a 747?
A Jet Setter.

What do you call a tiger with a machine gun?
Sir.

What does a tiger with a machine gun call you?
Dinner.

WHAT DO YOU CALL AN ALIEN THAT KNOWS LOTS OF JOKES?

I DON'T KNOW... BUT IF YOU DON'T STOP TELLING 'EM THEY'RE GOING TO HAVE TO CALL YOU AN AMBULANCE!

TELL ME WHY

I KNOW WHAT **I**'D LIKE TO ASK: WHY DO EARTHLINGS ASK SUCH RIDICULOUS QUESTIONS IN THE FIRST PLACE?

Why was Samson such a good entertainer?
Because he always brought the house down.

Why was Miss Piggy's boyfriend in court?
Because he'd kermit-ted an offence.

Why did the judge fine Tim Henman?
Because he caused a racket in court.

ARRGH! WOODY'S TELLING TENNIS JOKES... THAT'S NOT CRICKET!

Why did the porcupine like fashion shows?
Because he was a sharp dresser.

Why did the potatoes argue?
Because they couldn't see eye to eye.

Why are Saturday and Sunday so strong?
Because all the rest are weekdays.

Why did the burglar take a shower?
Because he wanted to make a clean getaway.

WHY DID THE CHICKEN CROSS THE ROAD?

OH NO! NOW WOODY'S KNICKERS ARE TELLING TERRIBLE JOKES!

THOSE AREN'T KNICKERS – THEY'RE A PAIR OF "WHY-FRONTS!"

Why is it cool to lose your temper? Because it's all the rage.

EEK! WHAT'S THE POINT OF HAVING YOUR HAIR DONE WHEN WOODY'S JOKES MAKE YOUR HAIR STAND ON END!

Why do monks like chips?
Because so many of them are friars.

Why do vampires like cheap cafés? Because they can eat for necks to nothing.

Why are hairdressers good drivers?
Because they know all the short cuts.

Why do fashion models put rollers in their hair before going to sleep?
So they can wake up curly in the morning.

Why don't they sell champagne in Boots?
Because it would leak through the laceholes.

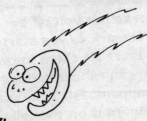

Why are you always scratching yourself?
Because no one else knows where I itch.

Why were the other animals pleased when the gnu left the zoo?
Because no gnus is good gnus.

WHY DID THE KETTLE WHISTLE?

BECAUSE IT WANTED TO LET OFF STEAM!

ACTUALLY I WAS WHISTLING FOR A TAXI TO GET ME AWAY FROM THIS AWFUL ALIEN!

Why are football
stadiums very cool?
Because they are
always full of fans.

Why did the professor
eat his dictionary?
*Because he wanted some
food for thought.*

Ultimate Joke
Telling Tip 7

If someone tries to put you off by
making a smart remark as you start
telling your joke, don't let them know
you're rattled. You can rehearse things
to say when this happens. For instance,
if someone says 'Heard it on the telly',
you can say 'Lucky you – now you're
going to hear it live'.

BUT YOU TOLD ME TO **SAY**
SOMETHING FUNNY...

YEAH. BUT THERE WAS
NO NEED TO SAY
"MY FACE"!

GOTCHAS!

I TRIED THESE OUT ON ALL MY ALIEN FRIENDS. THE ONLY TROUBLE IS, I DON'T HAVE ANY LEFT NOW!

What do you call very cold water?
Iced water.
What do you call very cold tea?
Iced tea.
What do you call very cold ink?
I know this one ... iced ink!
So I've noticed! Have you tried using a deodorant?

How do you keep a fool in suspense?
I don't know.
I'll tell you tomorrow.

WHY IS WOODY FROZEN IN THE ICE?

IT WAS THE ONLY WAY TO MAKE HIM CHILL OUT!

Have you got a good memory?
Of course I've got a good memory.
Knock, knock.
Who's there?
I thought you said you had a good memory?

I PREDICT THAT TOMORROW YOU WILL MEET A STRANGER... AND TELL THEM A TERRIBLE JOKE!

What do brainy people eat for lunch?
I don't know.
I didn't think you would.

Do you realize you've got a really nasty-looking boil on your neck?
What? Where?
Oh, I'm sorry – that's just your head.

Bet I can jump higher than a house.
Bet you can't.
I win. Houses can't jump.

Want to see a talking monkey?
Yes, please.
Take a look in the mirror then.

What's the difference between an elephant's bum and a postbox?
I don't know.
Well, I'm not sending you to post any letters.

WELL REALLY! I THINK EVEN WOODY CAN DO BETTER THAN TELL JOKES ABOUT ELEPHANTS' BOTTOMS!

OH I DON'T KNOW.. I QUITE LIKED IT!

Excuse me, sir, does your dog bite?
Of course not.
Here, boy...OUCH! Hey, I thought you
said your dog didn't bite?
He doesn't, but this isn't my dog.

Excuse me, are you a nose-picker?
Certainly not!
What a shame, because if you were
you'd have been able to pick a much
better-looking nose than the one
you've got.

FAMOUS FUNNIES

THERE ARE LOTS OF STARS IN THE UNIVERSE ... AND THIS LOT THAT WE'RE REALLY BRINGING DOWN TO EARTH!

Which film star is always jumping around the forest?
John Treevaulter.

What kind of football does James Bond play?
007-a-side.

How many ears does Captain Kirk have?
Three – a left one, a right one and a final frontier.

THEY'RE JOKES, CAPTAIN... BUT NOT AS WE KNOW THEM...

Who's big, grey and wrinkly and wears Blue Suede Shoes? *Elephants Presley.*

Who's fat and greedy and flies around the world? **Supperman.**

LOOK! UP IN THE SKY - IT'S A BIRD... IT'S A PLANE...

NO - IT'S A WOODY JOKE FALLING COMPLETELY FLAT!

Who's two foot tall and rides around the Wild West? *The Gnome Ranger.*

Who has the loudest stereo in Downing Street? *Tony Blare.*

Who are small, fat and wobbly and say 'eh-oh'? **The Jellytubbies.**

What's green and hairy and swings throught the jungle? Tarzan of the Grapes.

I SAY, I SAY I SAY...

LOOK! A STAND-UP COMET!

Ultimate Joke Telling Tip 8

Tell jokes that make everyone laugh – not jokes that make fun of other people. Otherwise you may find that the joke ends up being on you.

BUT NOT AS FLAT AS YOU'RE GOING TO BE...

THERE, THERE BABY HIPPO... MY JOKES ABOUT YOUR WEIGHT FELL A BIT FLAT...

DAFT DEFINITIONS

THESE MAD MEANINGS MIGHT NOT BE QUITE THE SAME AS THE ONES YOU'LL FIND IN AN EARTHLING DICTIONARY...

Aardvark
What your teacher makes you do

Acre
A very sore tooth

Boar
A pig which isn't very exciting

Butter
A bad-tempered goat

Chair
What people do after you shout 'Hip, hip ...'

Dance
The stupidest person in a very posh school

Each
Something you have to scratch or it will drive you crazy

Eavesdropper
What Adam's wife used when her eyes were sore

Fanatic
Where a football supporter keeps his old kit

Gargoyle
What Quasimodo does when he has a sore throat

Halo
What St Peter says when you turn up at the gates of heaven

Igloo
What Eskimos use to stick broken igs together

Jacket
What you do to a car with a flat tyre

Kilt
What you get if you accuse a big Scotsman of wearing a skirt

Leek
What you get when your spring onion is punctured

Magnet
What a newsagent uses to stop magazines falling off the shelves

Sausage
How old a hot dog is

Nag
A horse that complains a lot

Octopus
A cat with eight legs

Thick
What you get if you eat too much thupper

Parrots
The capital of France

Unsuitable
What you are if you can't buy clothes to fit

Quack
What duck eggs do if they're laid on concrete

Vest
Vot a wampire vears under his voolly jumper

Refugee
The one who blows the whistle when a gang of Ugees play football

Wicket
What you are when you hide someone's cricket bat

Yeti
What the Abominable Snowman dunks his biscuits in

Yellow
What scaredy cats do at the dentist

Zoo
What your English teacher would get a lawyer to do after reading this dictionary

WANT TO HEAR MY "DEFINITION" JOKES?

SORRY—I'M DEFINITELY LATE FOR AN APPOINTMENT!

DICTIONARY

WACKY WAITERS

I DON'T UNDERSTAND WHY EARTHLINGS COMPLAIN TO WAITERS ABOUT FLIES IN THEIR SOUP – I PAY EXTRA FOR THEM ON PLANET X!

'Waiter, waiter – there's a fly in my soup!'
'Not so loud, sir – everybody will want one!'

'Waiter, waiter – there's a fly in my soup!'
'Yes, sir – that's the meat.'

'Waiter, waiter – there's a fly in my soup!'
'Don't worry, sir – there are more than enough spiders in there to catch him!'

'Waiter, waiter – there's a fly in my soup!'
'What do you expect for a pound – smoked salmon?'

'Waiter, waiter – there's a fly in my soup!'
'Don't worry, sir – flies have very small appetites.'

'Waiter, waiter – there's a fly in my soup!'
'I'm sorry, sir – did you order a mosquito?'

'Waiter, waiter – there's a fly in my soup!'
'I'm sorry, sir – would you have liked it served separately?'

'Waiter, waiter – there's a fly in my soup!'
'Of course there is, sir – it's fly soup.'

'Waiter, waiter – there's a fly in my soup!'
'Don't worry, sir – we won't charge you any extra.'

WAITER! THERE'S A FLY IN MY SOUP!

PLEASE! DON'T TELL WOODY ALIEN OR HE'LL MAKE A TERRIBLE JOKE OUT OF IT!

'Waiter, waiter – there's a fly in my soup!'
'I'm sorry, sir – you should have told me you were a vegetarian.'

THIS IS THE ONLY CHANCE WOODY GETS TO TELL "SOUPER" JOKES...

SOUP

'Waiter, waiter – there's a spider in my soup!'
'Yes, sir – it's the fly's day off.'

'Waiter, waiter – there's a crocodile in my soup!'
'Well, sir, you told me to bring you lunch and make it snappy.'

'Waiter, waiter – this egg's gone off!'
'Don't blame me, sir – I only laid the table!'

'Waiter, waiter – do you have frogs' legs?'
'No, sir – I always walk like this.'

I TRIED BEING A COMEDIAN BUT IT'S NOT A JOB TO BE SNEEZED AT...

'Waiter, waiter – do you serve pork?'
'We're not fussy who we serve, sir – come right in.'

EVERYONE KNOWS CARROTS ARE GOOD FOR YOUR EYESIGHT... BUT WE'RE ALSO GOOD FOR EARS.. .. STICK US IN EACH ONE AND YOU WON'T HAVE TO LISTEN TO WOODY!

'Waiter, waiter – this coffee tastes like mud.'
'Yes, sir – it's just been ground.'

'Waiter, waiter – this food is terrible! Bring me the manager.'
'I don't think he'll taste much better, sir.'

'Waiter, waiter – this chicken tastes terrible.'
'Well, sir, you did ask for a foul dish.'

'Waiter, waiter – how long will my chips be?'
'About six centimetres each, I expect, sir.'

'Waiter, waiter – I don't like the look of this lobster.'
'I'm sorry, sir – do you want to eat it or marry it?'

'Waiter, waiter – there's a twig in my soup!'
'One moment, sir – I'll call the branch manager.'

'Waiter, waiter – there's a skull in my soup!'
'Yes, sir – it was cooked by the head chef.'

'Waiter, waiter – there's a bottom in my soup!'
'Yes, sir – the chef's got a little behind in his work.'

'Waiter, waiter – there's a car in my soup!'
'Yes, sir – it's Mini-strone.'

72

'Waiter, waiter – there's a fly in my soup!'
'Aren't you glad it's not half a fly, sir?'

'Waiter, waiter – there's a fly in my soup! What's it doing there?'
'Looks to me like the backstroke, sir.'

'Waiter, waiter – there's a fly in my soup!'
'Of course there is, sir – today's Flyday.'

'Waiter, waiter – there's a fly in my soup!'
'My mistake, sir – that soup belongs to the frog at the next table.'

WAITER! THERE'S A FLY IN MY SOUP!

NOT ANY MORE... IF YOU'RE GOING TO TELL TERRIBLE JOKES, I'M OFF!

'Waiter, waiter – there's a fly in my soup!'
'Don't worry, sir – that's just a beetle that does impressions.'

'Waiter, waiter – you've just knocked my dinner all over my lap!'
'Sorry, sir – but at least now you've got soup in your fly.'

Ultimate Joke Telling Tip 9

Always leave your audience wishing you had told more jokes – rather than wondering if you're ever going to stop!

HELP! I THOUGHT PEOPLE WERE SHOUTING "MORE, MORE!" NOT "MOWER, MOWER"...

I'LL CUT YOUR TERRIBLE ACT SHORT ONCE AND FOR ALL!

LAWN-O-MATIC

WHAT'S IN A NAME?

WE DON'T HAVE JOKES LIKE THESE ON PLANET X—PROBABLY BECAUSE THE MOST POPULAR NAME IS "PFFWRXXZZZYYIFFM!"

What do you call the man who reads the gas meter?
Bill.

What do you call a woman who hangs wet washing on a clothes line?
Peg.

What do you call a man who lifts up cars?
Jack.

What do you call a man who's always in church?
Neil.

What do you call a man with six rabbits down his trousers?
Warren.

HI-MY NAME IS WOODY ALIEN, AND I'M A COMEDIAN.

MY NAME IS GEORGE, I'VE HEARD YOUR JOKES AND IF YOU'RE A COMEDIAN, I'M A BANANA..

What do you call a woman who's full of holes?
Annette.

What do you call a man who's always dipping biscuits in his tea?
Duncan.

What do you call a woman who is small, green and round?
Olive.

What do you call a man who's always stealing anoraks?
Robin Hood.

DIPPY DOCTORS

AFTER THIS ROUND OF MEDICAL MADNESS, YOU'LL BE AS SICK AS A PARROT!

'Doctor, doctor – I've got a sore throat.'
'Stick your tongue out, please.'
'Why? Do you want to examine me?'
'No, it's just that I've got some stamps that need licking.'

'Doctor, doctor – how long can a person live without a brain?'
'I don't know – how old are you now?'

'Doctor, doctor – I've got just fifty-nine seconds to live!'
'Hold on, I'll be with you in a minute.'

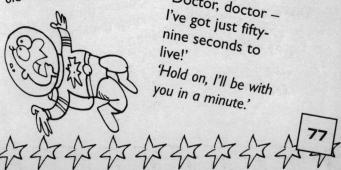

I'VE GOT TO GET TO A DOCTOR... WHILE, LISTENING TO WOODY'S JOKES I WENT DEAF IN ONE EAR!

GOOD IDEA! IF YOU HURRY, MAYBE YOU CAN GET THE DOCTOR TO BLOCK THE OTHER EAR!

'Doctor, doctor – the Invisible Man's outside.'
'Tell him I can't see him.'

'Doctor, doctor – how can I stop people ignoring me?'
'Next, please.'

'Doctor, doctor – what can you give me for water on the brain?'
'How about a tap on the head?'

'Doctor, doctor – I just can't stop lying.'
'I don't believe you.'

'Doctor, doctor – I keep thinking I'm a spoon.'
'Well, just sit there and don't stir.'

'Doctor, doctor – my wife thinks she's a clock.'
'Nonsense. She's just winding you up.'

'Doctor, doctor – everyone says I'm crazy just because I love sausages.'
'Of course you're not crazy – I like sausages, too.'
'Well, you must come and see my collection – I've got 2,000 of them!'

OPEN YOUR MOUTH WIDE AND STICK YOUR TONGUE OUT...

WHY? DO I LOOK ILL?

NO – I JUST WANT TO SHUT YOU UP FOR A BIT.

DOCTOR'S SURGERY

'Doctor, doctor – I keep thinking I'm a bumble bee.'
'Buzz off!'

'Doctor, doctor – I keep thinking I'm a broken pencil.'
'You're missing the point.'

'Doctor, doctor – I keep thinking I'm a kangaroo.'
'Hop it!'

'Doctor, doctor – I think I'm losing my memory.'
'How long has this been going on for?'
'How long has *what* been going on for?'

'Doctor, doctor –
I keep thinking I'm
a chicken.'
'How long have you
felt like this?'
'About six months.'
'Why didn't you
come to see me
before?'
'My family needed
the eggs.'

'Doctor, doctor –
I keep thinking I'm a
bridge.'
'What's come over
you.'
'Two cars, a bus and
an articulated lorry.'

'Doctor, doctor –
I keep seeing green
spots in front of my
eyes.'
'Have you seen a
psychiatrist?'
'No, just green
spots.'

'Doctor, doctor –
I'm having a lot
of pain from my
wooden leg.'
'How can that be?'
'My wife keeps
hitting me over
the head with it!'

'Doctor, doctor – I think I'm losing my memory.'
'You certainly are – you told me that a couple of jokes ago!'

'Doctor, doctor – I keep thinking I'm a cat.'
'How long have you thought that?'
'Ever since I was a kitten.'

'Doctor, doctor – my nose has gone red and I keep thinking I'm Rudolph.'
'Oh deer!'

I'M GETTING OUT OF HERE... SINCE WOODY STARTED DOING HIS ACT NOBODY NEEDS ME!

SLEEPING TABLETS

'Doctor, doctor – are these measles of mine catching?'
'Of course not ... now would you please move a bit further away?'

'Doctor, doctor – can you take my tonsils out?'
'Certainly. Would you rather I take them to the zoo or to the cinema?'

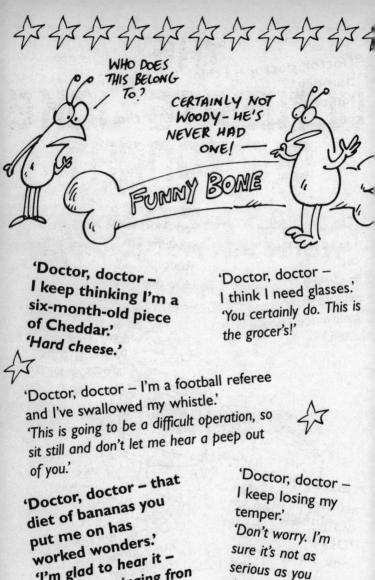

WHO DOES THIS BELONG TO?

CERTAINLY NOT WOODY – HE'S NEVER HAD ONE! –

FUNNY BONE

'Doctor, doctor –
I keep thinking I'm a
six-month-old piece
of Cheddar.'
'Hard cheese.'

'Doctor, doctor –
I think I need glasses.'
'You certainly do. This is
the grocer's!'

'Doctor, doctor – I'm a football referee
and I've swallowed my whistle.'
'This is going to be a difficult operation, so
sit still and don't let me hear a peep out
of you.'

'Doctor, doctor – that
diet of bananas you
put me on has
worked wonders.'
'I'm glad to hear it –
now stop swinging fron
the ceiling so I can
examine you.'

'Doctor, doctor –
I keep losing my
temper.'
'Don't worry. I'm
sure it's not as
serious as you
think.'
'OH YES IT IS,
YOU STUPID
LITTLE MAN!!!'

82

THE ULTIMATE JOKE DICTIONARY

An A-Z of the world's worst jokes ...

BEWARE – this dictionary will make grown men groan!

83

ARRGH! TERRIBLE
JOKES—I'M GETTING
OUT OF HERE
AS SOON AS
I'M "A"-BLE!

Acrobats
Did you hear the
one about the two
acrobats?
They fell head over
heels in love.

Aeroplane
What should you do if you
find an aeroplane on top
of your house?
Switch off the landing light.

MAYBE I
SHOULD BE
AN AEROPLANE—
AFTER ALL, MY
JOKES SEEM TO
GO OVER EVERYONES
— HEADS!

Air
What's the difference
between Woody Alien and
a balloon?
The balloon isn't always full of
hot air.

Ambition
'When I grow up
my ambition is to
be filthy rich.'
'Well, you've
managed the filthy bit
already.'

America

'Did you know Christopher Columbus discovered America?'
'No – in fact I didn't even know it was lost.'

Angel

Why was the angel in hospital?
He'd had a harp attack.

HEY. IS THIS HEAVEN?

BELIEVE ME, ANYWHERE FAR AWAY FROM WOODY AND HIS JOKES IS HEAVEN!

Arrow

When Robin Hood was dying, he raised himself from his bed one last time, put one last arrow in his bow and, drawing back the string with the last of his strength, told his Merry Men to bury him wherever the arrow landed. So he was buried on top of the wardrobe!

Astronauts

If athletes get tennis-elbow, do astronauts get missile-toe?

Aunts

How do you make anti-freeze?
Hide her woolly blanket.

B

Ball
What did one golf ball say to the other golf ball?
Meet you after tee.

Ballet
What do you get if your cross a pig with a ballerina?
Swine Lake.

Batman
Why are the police keeping an eye on Batman?
Because he never goes anywhere without Robin.

I'M LEAPING OUT OF HERE. THESE BALLET JOKES ARE TUTU MUCH!

Bus
'Excuse me, driver, does this bus stop at the seafront?'
'It had better or else there's going to be a really big splash!'

Butterflies
Why couldn't the butterfly go to the dance?
Because it was a mothball.

Bears
What do you call a teddy bear with BO?
Winnie-the-Phew.

Bees
Why do bees have sticky hair?
Because they use honeycombs.

HAVE YOU HEARD ABOUT THE POLAR BEAR WHO TRIED TO TELL WOODY'S JOKES? THEY GOT A FROSTY RECEPTION!

Bone
Where's the best place to find dinosaur bones?
Wherever the dinosaur dog has buried them.

IF THIS IS THE STANDARD OF HUMOUR, IT'S TIME FOR ME TO "B" SOMEWHERE ELSE!

Bucket
How can you tell if a bucket is sick?
See if it's a little pail.

Camera

'Doctor, doctor – I've swallowed the film from my camera. Is that serious?'
'I don't know – we'll have to wait and see what develops.'

MY ACT IS VERY EASY TO PHOTOGRAPH – ONCE I START THE AUDIENCE IS GONE IN A — FLASH!

Card

What did the Mummy Playing Card say to the Baby Playing Card?
'Stand up straight and stop shuffling around.'

Cat

FIRST NEIGHBOUR: I'm afraid I've just knocked over your cat and I'd like to replace it.
SECOND NEIGHBOUR: Well, we've got mice in the kitchen, so get busy.

YUK! YOU WON'T "C" ME LISTENING TO JOKES LIKE THIS FOR MUCH LONGER!

88

Chores

CHILD: Mum, would you punish me for something I didn't do?
MUM: Of course not.
CHILD: Good. I didn't do the dishes.

Christmas

FIRST NEIGHBOUR: We're going to get a dog for Christmas.
SECOND NEIGHBOUR: Really? We're having turkey, same as last year.

WHAT'S THE DIFFERENCE BETWEEN ONE OF WOODY'S GAGS AND A CHRISTMAS STOCKING?

CHRISTMAS STOCKINGS DON'T USUALLY STINK!

Climbing

FIRST CLIMBER: Is it dangerous on top of this mountain?
SECOND CLIMBER: Not at all – it's only when they hit the bottom that people get hurt.

Coins

'Doctor, doctor – my son's swallowed a pound coin!'
'Why on earth did he do that?'
'I gave it to him and told him it was for his lunch.'

Cowboy

Why did the cowboy buy a fridge freezer?
Because he wanted to be quick on the thaw.

Cows

What do cows shout when they go bungee-jumping?
'Geronimoo!'

D

Dad

TEACHER: Did your father help you with your homework?
PUPIL: No, I got it wrong all by myself.

Demon

Why did the demon learn to play the harp? Because neither of his horns was working.

Dandruff

What's a guaranteed cure for dandruff? Baldness.

HERE'S A HOT TIP...

WOODY'S A HELL OF A BAD COMEDIAN!

Diets

My big sister went on a coconut diet. She hasn't lost any weight, but you should see her climb trees!

Dinosaurs

What's very loud and keeps cavemen awake at night? Dino-snores.

THEY TOLD ME THIS WAS A JOKE BOOK... BUT I THINK I'VE BEEN "D"-CEIVED!

Dogs

FIRST DOG: Where do fleas go in winter?
SECOND DOG: Search me!

Doll

BOY: I'd like a doll for my little sister.
SHOP ASSISTANT: I'm sorry, we don't do swaps.

WHAT'S THE BEST WAY TO BE A WATCHDOG?

WATCH OUT FOR WOODY'S TERRIBLE JOKES!

Doughnut

Have you heard the one about the giant doughnut?
Yes, but I found it a bit hard to swallow.

Draughts

My dad's very good at draughts — whenever he plays he leaves all the doors and windows open.

E

Easter
What does Santa Claus do at Easter?
He egg-nores the whole thing.

Echo
'There's a very strong echo around here.'
'You can say that again.'

Eel
Why did the electric eel complain in the restaurant?
Because he'd been overcharged.

Elvis
Why did Elvis switch off his alarm clock?
He wanted to have a blue suede snooze.

Eggs
FIRST MAN: Why have you got two fried eggs on your head?
SECOND MAN: Because the boiled ones keep rolling off.

Entrance
Why did Sherlock Holmes paint his front door like a daffodil?
It was a yellow entry, my dear Watson.

LOOK, I'VE GOT A FAN LETTER!

IS IT A NICE ONE?

I HOPE SO - IT TOOK ME AGES TO WRITE!

Envelope

What did one envelope say to the other envelope?

'You stamp on me and I'll give you a terrible licking!'

Exams

FIRST PUPIL: How were the exam questions?

SECOND PUPIL: Fine. It was the answers I had trouble with.

WHAT GHASTLY GAGS! LUCKY THIS BOOK HAS AN "E-JECTOR" SEAT!

Excuses

PUPIL: Hello.

TEACHER: I'm phoning to say I won't be able to come to school today.

TEACHER: Why not?

PUPIL: I've lost my voice.

"E

BOING!

93

Farms

YOUNG FARMER: Can you tell me how long cows should be milked?

OLD FARMER: Same way as short cows.

IF I COULD ESCAPE FROM THIS BOOK I REALLY WOULD BE OVER THE MOON!

Feet

'Doctor, doctor – I've got flat feet.'
'Have you tried a foot pump?'

Fire brigade

A fire engine was racing towards an emergency with all its sirens blaring. But as the fire-fighters looked out of the window they could see a little man jogging along beside them. They turned the engine to full throttle and the sirens to full blast, but no matter how fast they went the little man was still there, running along beside them.

Finally the driver stuck his head out of the window and shouted, 'Why are you following us? What do you want?'

'Two cones, a ninety-nine and a can of cola, please!'

Flower

What do you get if you cross a spotted dog with a bunch of flowers?
101 Carnations.

I'M MAKING A BIG "F-FORT" TO GET OUT OF HERE!

Fly

Why do flies buzz?
Because their front door key isn't working.

Frankenstein

Why did Frankenstein's monster have indigestion?
He was always bolting his food.

Food

FIRST WOMAN: I've just found this great new restaurant where you can eat dirt cheap.
SECOND WOMAN: Yeah, but who wants to eat dirt?

Fridge

Why did the fridge-maker go bankrupt?
Business wasn't so hot.

Frog

DAD: Why did you put a live frog in your sister's bed?
SON: Because I couldn't find a dead mouse.

I WAS GOING TO TELL A REALLY GOOD JOKE — BUT I FROG-GOT THE PUNCHLINE!

Ghost
Why did the ghost jump into a vat of ice-cream? Because he wanted to walk through Walls.

Gifts
Why do wooden legs make good Christmas presents? Because they are excellent stocking fillers.

Giant
Why was the giant covered in tomato sauce? He'd just climbed up a baked bean -stalk.

FEE, FI, FO, FUM ... I SMELL JOKES THAT ARE REALLY DUMB!

Giraffe
Did you hear about the giraffe who wanted to be a comedian? He'd been told it took an awful lot of neck.

Glass
PUPIL: Please, Miss, can I have a glass of water?
TEACHER: No, Johnny. That's the fourth one you've asked for in one lesson. Why do you want so many glasses of water anyway?
PUPIL: I'm trying to stop the fire spreading to the rest of the school.

Gloves
GIRL: Hey – you've got your gloves on the wrong hands!
BOY: But these are the only hands I have.

Goldfish

MUM: Why haven't you given the goldfish fresh water?

DAUGHTER: Because they haven't drunk the water I gave them yesterday.

IS IT TRUE THAT ALL GOLDFISH HAVE SHORT MEMORIES?

WELL, WE KNOW WHEN WE'VE HEARD BAD JOKES BEFORE!

Gorilla

A big gorilla came into the corner shop and asked for a bar of chocolate.

'Th-that'll be fifty pence, please,' the shopkeeper stammered as he handed over the chocolate. 'You know, this is the f-first time we've ever had a gorilla in this shop...'

'Don't worry,' said the gorilla. 'At fifty pence for a bar of chocolate, it'll be the last.'

Grass

Who rides a white horse and is very good at cutting grass? The Lawn Arranger.

GEE WHIZZ! I THINK IT'S TIME FOR THIS "G" TO WHIZZ TO WHERE SOMETHING FUNNY'S HAPPENING!!

97

H

Hair
BOY: Aarrgh! Look at the state of my hair!
FRIEND: But you said you wanted it cut like Leonardo DiCaprio's.
BOY: Yes, but Leo doesn't have his hair cut like this!
FRIEND: He does if he lets me do it.

Hands
'Would you like your palm read?'
'No thanks – I'd prefer it to be the same colour it's always been.'

Headmaster
HEADMASTER: What's your name?
PUPIL: Malcolm Robinson.
HEADMASTER: You're supposed to say 'Sir'.
PUPIL: OK, Sir Malcolm Robinson.

Hardware shop
CUSTOMER: Have you got six-inch nails?
ASSISTANT: Yes, madam.
CUSTOMER: Well, would you scratch my back, please. It's really itchy.

Heat
TEACHER: Heat makes things expand and cold makes them contract.
PUPIL: So that's why the days are longer in summer and shorter in winter!

I KEEP TELLING WOODY TO QUIT COMEDY – BUT IT'S LIKE BANGING MY HEAD AGAINST A BRICK WALL!

Horse

'Doctor, doctor, my brother thinks he's a horse. Can you cure him?'

'Yes, but it'll cost a lot of money.'

'That's no problem – he's just won the Grand National.'

I TRIED TO SWITCH FROM SHOW JUMPING TO COMEDY... BUT THE LACK OF GOOD GAGS WAS A BIT OF A HURDLE!

Help

A bishop was walking down the street when a small boy called for help.

'Please, sir, I can't reach this doorbell. Would you ring it for me?'

'Certainly,' said the bishop and did as he was asked. 'Now, is there anything else I can do?'

'Yes – run like hell!'

Hyena

Have you heard about the hyena who lost his voice?

Yes – it was no laughing matter.

Hiccups

What colour is a hiccup? Burple.

I'M ONE LETTER WHO'S GOING TO BE WRITING A LETTER... OF COMPLAINT ABOUT THESE DREADFUL JOKES!

99

Ink
'Have you heard the joke about invisible ink?'
'Of course not – it was written on a blank sheet of paper!'

Ig
FIRST PUPIL: Hang on…what *is* an Ig?
SECOND PUPIL: It's an Eskimo's house without a loo.

I-Spy
BOY: I spy with my little eye something beginning with 'T'.
GIRL: Breakfast.
BOY: Breakfast doesn't begin with 'T'.
GIRL: You're right … sometimes I have orange juice.

OOER! WOODY'S STILL TELLING JOKES! "ICE" SUPPOSE I'LL STAY IN HERE A BIT LONGER!

Illness
What illness do ex-pilots get?
Flu.

Imitations
GIRL: My brother can do great bird imitations.
BOY: You mean he can copy their voices?
GIRL: No – he eats worms.

India
Why should moggies stay away from Indian restaurants?
Because curry-osity killed the cat.

Indiana Jones

What do you get if you cross Indiana Jones with a carton of milk?
Whipped cream.

HAVING TO LISTEN TO STUFF LIKE THIS IS "ONE IN THE I" FOR ME!!

Itching

What happened to the clown who lost his itching powder?
He had to start again from scratch.

Ireland

Knock, knock.
Who's there?
Irish Stew.
Irish Stew who?
Irish Stew in the name of the law.

GOSH! A LUCKY IRISH LEPRECHAUN!

AND I'LL BE EVEN LUCKIER IF I GET OUT OF HERE BEFORE YOUR ACT STARTS!

Jacket
FIRST PUPIL: Why did you set fire to your jacket?
SECOND PUPIL: I've always wanted a blazer.

Jack-in-the-Box
What do Jack-in-the-Boxes like reading?
Pop-up books.

Jam
Have you heard the joke about the strawberry jam?
Yes – but please don't spread it around.

Jelly
What did the jelly do when it fell out of its bowl?
It threw a wobbly.

– ANY MORE BAD JELLY JOKES AND THIS BOOK WILL BE DESSERT-ED!

I MAY BE SHAPED LIKE A HOOK BUT I WISH I HADN'T BEEN HOOKED INTO TELLING THESE CRUMMY "J" JOKES!

Jewellery
What did the diamond sing when it went to a football match?
'Jewel never walk alone.'

Jockey
Where do you take a sick jockey?
To a horse-pital.

Journey
FIRST HIKER: How far are we from the next town?
SECOND HIKER: About ten miles.
FIRST HIKER: Oh, good – that's only five miles each.

Joke
Have you heard the new joke about binmen?
Yes – it's a load of old rubbish.

Jungle
What do you call a polar bear in the jungle?
Lost.

YOU KNOW, I FOUND WOODY'S JUNGLE JOKE QUITE AMUSING!

IGNORE HIM READERS— HE'S OUT OF HIS TREE!

K

I WENT FOR A JOB AT A COMEDY CLUB BUT THEY'D ONLY LET ME BE A BOUNCER!

Kangaroo
What does a kangaroo get on its birthday?
Many Hoppy Returns.

Kidney
What do pythons like for dinner?
Snake and kidney pie.

King
Why did Old King Cole like having his feet tickled?
He wanted to have merry old soles.

Kayak
Why did the Eskimo set fire to his boat?
Because he wanted to have his kayak and eat it.

Kipper
Why do fish never lose football matches?
Because they've got a very good goalkipper.

Kiss

FROG: Kiss me, beautiful princess, for I was not always a frog.
PRINCESS: What were you before, then?
FROG: A tadpole.

YECCH! IF THIS IS THE STANDARD OF JOKE AROUND HERE, I'M HOPPING IT BACK TO MY PAD!

Kite

Have you heard the joke about the kite?
Yes — it really blew me away.

Knight

Why were the Middle Ages called the Dark Ages?
Because there were so many knights.

Knot

GIRL: Want to hear a great joke about knots?
BOY: Sorry, I'm tied up at the moment.

I'M GOING TO TEAM UP WITH LETTER "O"... AND K.O. THAT ALIEN FOR ROPING ME INTO HIS TERRIBLE DICTIONARY!

L

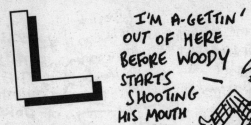

I'M A-GETTIN' OUT OF HERE BEFORE WOODY STARTS SHOOTING HIS MOUTH OFF!

Lasso

Why was the cowboy no good with his lasso?
Because nobody had shown him the ropes.

Laziness

My uncle's so lazy he won't even go outside to see if it's raining. He just calls the dog in and checks if it's wet.

Lancelot

Why was Sir Lancelot always sleepy?
He was on the knight shift.

Life

I hope I live to be 110, because you don't hear of many people dying after that age.

EEK! WHAT THE "L" AM I DOING HERE?!

Lion
Have you heard the joke about the lion?
Yes – it really made me roar!

Lipstick
I'd like to buy my mum some lipstick for her birthday, only I'm not sure what size her mouth is.

Loo
How can you tell when your loo's embarrassed?
It looks a bit flushed.

HOW LONG ARE YOU GOING TO STAY LOCKED IN THERE?

FOR AS LONG AS YOU'RE GOING TO KEEP TELLING JOKES OUT THERE!

London
Who was London's stupidest Lord Mayor?
Thick Whittington.

Liquorice
FIRST BOY: I love liquorice, don't you?
SECOND BOY: No, I can't stand it.
FIRST BOY: Oh, well – I suppose it takes allsorts.

MAYBE WOODY SHOULD SWITCH TO BEING A MAGICIAN? HIS JOKES ALWAYS MAKE THE AUDIENCE DISAPPEAR!

Magic

Did you hear about the magician's assistant who got tired of getting sawn in half? She left him and is now living happily in North and South America.

Meals

PUPIL: Can I have my school dinner completely overcooked, on a dirty plate with a big greasy thumbprint in the mashed potato?
SCHOOL COOK: I couldn't possibly serve you a meal like that.
PUPIL: Why not? You did yesterday.

Mind-readers

What did one mind-reader say to the other mind-reader?
'You're fine. How am I?'

Moon

Why are parties on the Moon so boring?
There's no atmosphere.

Morning

Why should you wake up with a joke every morning?
Because it's the crack of dawn.

Mouse

What do you sing to a mouse on his birthday?
'For cheese a jolly good fellow!'

WOODY'S NOT MUCH OF A COMEDIAN...

...BUT SOMEHOW IT DOESN'T SEEM TO HAVE DAWNED ON HIM!

Moses

How did Moses part the Red Sea?
With a sea-saw.

Motorbike

What do you get if you cross a white rabbit with a motorbike?
Alice in Hondaland.

Music

Why did Mozart stay in bed all day?
He wanted to write sheet music.

MMMM-MUM!! SAVE ME FROM THIS ALIEN AWFULNESS!

Navy

SAILOR: Why are you so angry, Admiral? You told me to drop the anchor!

ADMIRAL: Yes — but not on my foot!

Nest

What notice did the sparrow put in a frame over his nest?

'Home, Tweet Home.'

New York

Where do New York bats hang out?

At the Vampire State Building.

Night

What happened when the ghost punctured his bicycle tyre?

He was a thing that went 'pump' in the night.

Nile

Why couldn't Tutankhamen go swimming in the Nile?

Because he hadn't got permission from his mummy.

News

We've just heard that a large hole has been discovered in the middle of Wembley football stadium. The police are reported to be looking into it.

MY JOKES WOULD FIT VERY WELL IN THIS JOKEBOOK! MOST OF THEM ARE 5,000 YEARS OLD!

North Pole

What kind of mints do Arctic explorers eat?
North Polos.

Nose

How do you stop your nose running?
Take away its jogging shoes.

Nuts

Why wouldn't the nut sit on the fence?
Because it was a walnut.

O

Oak
Why did the oak tree make a New Year's Resolution? Because it wanted to turn over a new leaf.

PROTECT THE FOREST! DON'T FORCE IT TO LISTEN TO WOODY JOKES!

Ocean
Why did the ocean blush? Because the seaweed.

I'D BE A VERY GOOD COMEDIAN – I'D HAVE THE AUDIENCE IN KNOTS!

Octopus
'Doctor, doctor, I think I'm an octopus.'
'Don't worry – I can help you.'
'Are you sure or are you just pulling my leg, leg, leg, leg, leg, leg, leg, leg?'

Oil

What jumps up and down inside a barrel shouting 'Knickers!'
Crude oil.
What jumps up and down inside a barrel shouting 'Underwear!'
Refined oil.

Onions

FIRST COOK: Ouch! These onions are making my eyes smart.
SECOND COOK: Better rub some on your head, then.

WHOEVER GOT ME INTO THIS BOOK 'O'S ME A BIG APOLOGY!

Orange

Why don't judges peel oranges before eating them?
Because they want the fruit, the whole fruit and nothing but the fruit.

Outback

What's red and green and hops round the outback?
Kanga-rhubarb.

Owl

What do you call an owl with no beak?
Anything you like – it doesn't give a hoot.

Oz

What's green and slimy and crawls down the Yellow Brick Road?
The Lizard of Oz.

113

P

Pet shop
CUSTOMER: Have you got any kittens going cheap?
ASSISTANT: No, all our kittens go miaow.

HOWL! I'VE NEVER HEARD JOKES AS BAD AS THESE IN ALL MY NINE LIVES!

Park
I went for a job as a litter collector in my local park. They asked me if I wanted training but I told them I'd pick it up as I went along.

Pants
FIRST BOY: Have you got any holes in your pants?
SECOND BOY: Certainly not!
FIRST BOY: Then how do you get your legs through?

Piano
PARENT: Why are you banging your head on that piano?
CHILD: I'm trying to play by ear.

Pig
Why is Woody Alien like a pig?
Because he can be a bit of a boar.

Pipe
What did the pipe say to the drill?
'Oil be seeing you.'

NEVER MIND
'ELLO, ELLO, ELLO —
WITH WOODY'S
JOKES IT'S —
GOODBYE,
GOODBYE,
GOODBYE!

Police
What did the policeman say to his stomach?
'Don't move – I've got you under a vest.'

Professor
Why did the nutty professor put a knocker on his door?
He wanted to win the Nobel Prize.

Problem
'Doctor, doctor, can you help me out?'
'Certainly. Which way did you come in?'

PETER PIPER MAY
HAVE PICKED A
PECK OF PICKLED
PEPPERS... BUT
WHY DID THAT
AWFUL ALIEN
HAVE TO PICK
JOKES LIKE
THESE?

Q

Quack
Why do ducks quack?
Because they haven't been glued together pwoperly.

Quake
What do you call a cow in an earthquake?
A milkshake.

QUICK SHOW ME THE 'Q' — FOR THE EXIT!!

Quasimodo
Where does Quasimodo keep his pet rabbits?
In a hutch, back of Notre-Dame.

Queen
What does the Queen do in bad weather?
She puts on her reign coat.

Quiet
Why did the chef stick frozen vegetables in his ears?
Because he wanted some peas and quiet.

Quilt
Why did the policeman buy a big quilt for his bed?
Because he wanted to be an undercover cop.

Quill
Why did William Shakespeare write with a quill pen?
The feather tickled his fancy.

Quote
TEACHER: Who said, 'To be or not to be …'?
PUPIL: You did, sir, just then.

Quiz
SALESMAN: Congratulations! You've won two return tickets to America.
CUSTOMER: But I don't want to go twice.

OF COURSE, I DON'T JUST TELL JOKES... I CAN ALSO DO TRAGEDY!

HAMLET

THE WAY YOU TELL JOKES IS A TRAGEDY!

R

Rabbits
Where do rabbits get their glasses?
From the hoptician.

Race
How do you start a teddy-bear race?
'Ready, teddy, go!'

Raffle
TICKET SELLER: Would you like to buy a raffle ticket for our local hospital?
WOMAN IN STREET: Certainly not! What would I do with it if I won?

Railways
TRAVELLER: I'd like a return ticket, please.
ASSISTANT: Certainly, sir. Where to?
TRAVELLER: Back here of course!

UGH!
IF WOODY LOST HIS JOKE BOOK I'D BE
— WELL CHUFFED!

WHY OH WHY "R" YOU STILL READING? HAVE YOU NO SENSE OF PAIN??!

Robber

FIRST BOY: But you can't be a robber when you grow up – that's dangerous!
SECOND BOY: No, it's all right. I'm going to be a safe-robber.

River

Where do ducks keep their money?
In a river bank.

Roads

Where do road-menders fry their sausages?
On a pneumatic grill.

Rock

Two rocks – which one was braver, the big one or the small one?
The small one – it was just a little boulder.

Restaurant

WAITER: How did you find your steak sir?
CUSTOMER: I looked under the lettuce and there it was.

I DON'T KNOW MANY JOKES BUT I'VE GOT SOME SIZZLING ONE-LINERS!

School

I like going to school and I like coming home. The only bit I don't like is the bit in between.

Skunk

How do you know when a skunk's gone off?
It's past its 'smell-by' date.

PEOPLE WHO THINK I STINK – OBVIOUSLY HAVEN'T HEARD WOODY'S ACT.

Sleep

'Doctor, doctor – I'm having trouble sleeping. What should I do?'
'Lie on the edge of the bed – you'll soon drop off.'

Star Trek

How many trees are there aboard the Starship Enterprise?
Only one – the captain's log.

Snake

What do snakes use to keep the rain off their cars?
Windscreen vipers.

Socks

'Have you ever told a joke about a sock?'
'I tried to, but I kept putting my foot in it.'

Soup

'Waiter, waiter — this soup tastes disgusting!'
'What are you complaining about? You've only got a bowl, whereas we've got a whole pot of the stuff.'

SSSSEE YOU LATER... IT'S TIME I WAS SSOMEWHERE ELSE!

Spiders

Where do spiders play football?
Webley Stadium.

Swimming

My brother had a go at swimming the English Channel, but he turned back halfway because he didn't think he'd make it.

Tap-dancing

I had to give up tap-dancing – I kept falling in the sink.

Telephone

CALLER: Hello, Headmaster, I'm phoning to say Maxine won't be at school today.
HEADMASTER: Who is this calling?
CALLER: This is my mother.

Time

GIRL: What time is it?
SISTER: Five o'clock.
GIRL: I don't believe you.
SISTER: Why not?
GIRL: Because when I asked you this morning you gave me a different answer.

Toad
Where do toads put their anoraks?
In the croak room.

Toilet
Who invented the toilet?
I don't know, but I'm sure he was flushed with success.

Toe
What did one toe say to the other toe?
'You're getting too big for your boots.'

Tools
Why are nails no good at playing football?
Their team keeps getting hammered.

Trousers
Why is a tailor always out of breath?
Because he works among lots of trousers and pants.

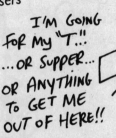

I'M GOING FOR MY "T"... ...OR SUPPER... OR ANYTHING TO GET ME OUT OF HERE!!

U

Udders
Why are dairy farmers such nice people? Because they're always thinking of udders.

Ugly
BROTHER: I bet I can make an uglier face than you.
SISTER: Yes – but you've got a head start!

Ukelele
Did you hear about the vampire who played the banjo?
No, but I heard about the ghost who played the spook-ulele.

COME OUT – THE WORST OF THE JOKES ARE OVER!

NO WAY! I'M WAITING TILL THE GHOST IS CLEAR!

Uncle

Why did old
Uncle Albert hide
his wife's
bloomers?
He wanted to make
Auntie Freeze.

Underground

What do you call a
crowd of dentists
on the London
Underground?
A toothpaste tube.

Under the sea

What lies at the
bottom of the
ocean and quivers?
A nervous wreck.

Unicorn

What did one
unicorn say to the
other?
You've got a very good
point there.

Unicycle

Who invented the
unicycle?
I don't know, but it
was a wheely good
idea.

Usher

I took my seat in
the cinema, but the
usher made me put
it back.

IF THIS IS
THE BEST OF
THE EARTH'S
"U" JOKES, ITS
TIME I
MADE A
U-TURN!

125

V

Vacuum cleaner
What did one vacuum cleaner say to the other vacuum cleaner? *'Do you take me for a sucker?'*

Vampire
What do you call a vampire that's always feeling peckish? Snackula.

Vampire bat
Why do vampires change into bats? *Because they're wicket creatures.*

PSST! "V" VERE VONDERING IF YOU MIGHT KNOW THE VAY OUT OF HERE?

Vase
MUM: Oh no! That vase you've just broken has been in our family for years!
SON: Phew! Good job it wasn't a new one.

Vest
What did the vest say to the chest? *'Don't move! I've got you covered.'*

Violet

Have you heard the joke about the violet?

You won't like it at first, but after a while it will grow on you.

I'M NOT NORMALLY A SHRINKING VIOLET, BUT SINCE WOODY ALIEN LANDED HERE, THE WHOLE PLANET'S GONE TO POT!

Vet

'Vet, vet – my dog's got no nose!'

'How does he smell?'

'Terrible!'

Violin

Why should you never buy a second-hand violin?

Because it might be a fiddle.

Viper

Why did the viper give his teacher an apple?

Because he was a terrible crawler.

W

Wafer
What did one ice-cream cone say to the other ice-cream cone?
'Wafer me!'

Wade
CHILD: Mum, come quick! Dad waded out to sea and now he's up to his ankles in the water!
MUM: That's not very dangerous.
CHILD: It is when he's upside down.

Watch
What goes, 'Tick, tick, woof'?
A watch dog.

YUM, YUM! I'LL HAVE AN ICE CREAM PLEASE...

EEK! I DON'T KNOW ABOUT YOU, BUT "ICE CREAM" EVERY TIME YOU GET YOUR JOKEBOOK OUT!

Werewolf
When do werewolves go trick or treating?
Howl-oween.

Whale
How do you tell how heavy a whale is?
Take it to a whale-weigh station.

Wig

FIRST MAN: Do you know any jokes about wigs?
SECOND MAN: Not off the top of my head.

Wind

What did one wind say to the other wind? Nothing – they immediately came to blows.

LOOK, THERE'S BEEN A MISTAKE ... I'M ACTUALLY AN "M" UPSIDE DOWN SO I'LL GET ÒERS OUT OF HERE, RIGHT NOW...

Worm

Why was the swallow grumpy every morning? It wanted to be the surly bird that catches the worm.

Winter

Why do birds fly south in winter? Because if they walked they wouldn't get there till spring.

X

Two fishermen were at sea when they found a really good spot for catching fish. They stayed out as long as they could, but as night began to fall they had to return to shore.

'What a pity,' said the first fisherman. 'We'll never be able to find this spot again.'

'Of course we will,' said the other. 'I've painted an "X" on the side of the boat!'

I DON'T WISH TO CARP BUT THESE JOKES ARE TERRIBLE!

IN WOODY'S HANDBOOK WHAT DID YOU X-PECT?

X Certificate

CINEMA MANAGER: You can't come in – this is an over-eighteen movie!

GIRL: That's OK – I've brought nineteen of my friends!

X-Files
How do monsters keep their nails in good condition? They use their X-files.

X-ray
'Doctor, doctor, I keep thinking I'm an X-ray.'
'Stop trying to fool me! I can see right through you!'

X-ray specs
LITTLE BROTHER: Wow! These X-ray specs really work!
SISTER: Oh, don't be so ridiculous.
LITTLE BROTHER: I wasn't talking to you. I was talking to the person in the next room.

I DON'T KNOW WHY I'M JUST ON THIS PAGE... THE WHOLE BOOK SHOULD HAVE AN 'X' CERTIFICATE!

Xylophone
Where do xylophone players get their hair cut? On top of their heads, same as everyone else.

XXXYYLXMXXXLLLLMXXXXXYXXXXX!
There was a big football match on the planet Mars and one of the Martian players tripped his opponent in the penalty area.

'Right,' said the referee, 'I'm booking you for that. What's your name?'

'XXXYYLXMXXXLLLLMXXXXXYXXXXX.'
'On second thoughts, I'll let you off with a warning.'

Yacht

SAILOR: Do you want your lunch now?
PASSENGER: No, just throw it over the side and save time.

Yak

What was the yak's favourite TV show?
The Six o'Clock Gnus.

Year

What did 31st December say to 1st January?
'Year we go again.'

DON'T YOU GET SICK OF HEARING WOODY'S JOKES?

NO - I JUST LET THEM GO IN ONE YEAR AND OUT THE OTHER!

Yeast

Why did the ghost put yeast in his coffin?
He wanted to rise again.

Y, OH Y HAVE I GOT TO PUT UP WITH JOKES LIKE THIS?

Yellow
Why are bananas yellow?
Because if you give them a little squeeze, they jump out of their skins.

Yeti
What do you get if you cross a tortoise with a yeti?
An Abominable Slowman.

Yoke
Did you hear the one about the yellow part of an egg?
Yes, but I just didn't get the yoke.

Yodel
Who skis around the Swiss Alps and chases Daleks?
Dr Yodel-ay-hee-Who.

Yule
Where does Santa keep his Yule logs?
In his yule-ery box.

WHAT WOULD YOU LIKE FOR CHRISTMAS?

NOTHING — I JUST WANT SOMEONE TO TAKE YOU AND YOUR ROTTEN GAGS AWAY!

133

Zebra
What do zebras have for breakfast?
Stripes Krispies.

Zebra crossing
What goes, 'Now you see me, now you don't. Now you see me, now you don't'?
A penguin on a zebra crossing.

Zinc
What happened when the chemistry teacher fell off the pier?
He had to zinc or swim.

Zip
'Doctor, doctor, I keep thinking I'm a zip fastener!'
'You really should pull yourself together.'

Zombie
Why was the zombie thrown out of school?
Because he was always dead late.

HONESTLY TEACHER – A DOG ATE MY BONEWORK!

Zero

Have you heard about the two zeros who got married? They wanted to tie the nought.

Zoo

FIRST GIRL: I went to the zoo last Saturday.

SECOND GIRL: What a coincidence. I was there on Saturday too.

FIRST GIRL: That's strange. I looked in all the cages and I didn't see you …

Zookeeper

FIRST MAN: Have you heard about the zookeeper who liked to tickle the tiger's chin with his right hand?

SECOND MAN: No – what was his name?

FIRST MAN: Lefty.

ZZZZZZZ

…AND SO ANOTHER LUCKY LETTER ENJOYS MY WONDERFUL SENSE OF HUMOUR…

ZZZZZZZZ

WELL, I'VE TRIED EVERY POSSIBLE EARTH JOKE AND I DIDN'T GET ANY MORE LAUGHS THEN USUAL...

I MIGHT AS WELL GO BACK TO PLANET X...

PLEASE! ON BEHALF OF ALL OF US ON PLANET X IF YOU KNOW ANY EARTH JOKES WOODY HASN'T TRIED YET, SEND THEM IN SO WE CAN SEND HIM BACK TO EARTH FOR HIS NEXT BOOK!

READ MORE IN PUFFIN

The Rabbit
and the Crab

by Amelia Marshall and Roman Diaz

FRANKLIN WATTS

LONDON•SYDNEY

Long ago, Rabbit and Crab
were good friends.
One day, they wanted to grow
some carrots.

"I will plant the seeds," said Rabbit.

"And I will water them," said Crab.

Soon the carrots were ready to pick.

Rabbit dug up the carrots and

Crab cut off the tops.

Before long, there was a little pile
of carrots and big pile of carrot tops.

Rabbit wanted to trick Crab.

"I have an idea," he said to Crab.

"You can have the big pile.

I will have the little pile."

But Crab was clever.

"No, Rabbit," she said.

"Then you will have all the carrots."

"Then let's have a race," said Rabbit.

"The winner has the carrots.

The loser has the tops."

"Okay," said Crab.

Rabbit was happy.

"I can run very fast," he thought.

"Crab is too slow to beat me."

11

"I can run faster than you,"
Rabbit said to Crab. " So I will start
ten steps behind you."

"Okay," said Crab.

"You are much faster than me."

They got ready to start the race.

Crab stood by the starting line.

"Ready, steady, go!" she shouted.

Rabbit ran fast and soon
he ran past Crab.

Rabbit ran and ran.

He could not see Crab.

"I am going to win," he thought.

But clever Crab was holding on

to Rabbit's tail with her claws.

17

Rabbit ran up to the pile of carrots.

Crab jumped down.

"I got here first," said Crab.

"I won the race."

"Oh no," cried Rabbit.

"You tricked me!"

So, Rabbit lost the race
and Crab ate all the carrots.

Story order

Look at these 5 pictures and captions.
Put the pictures in the right order
to retell the story.

1

Rabbit lets Crab start the race in front.

2

Rabbit suggests having a race.

3

Crab holds on to Rabbit's tail.

4

Rabbit and Crab plant some carrots.

5

Rabbit has an idea.

Independent Reading

This series is designed to provide an opportunity for your child to read on their own. These notes are written for you to help your child choose a book and to read it independently.

In school, your child's teacher will often be using reading books which have been banded to support the process of learning to read. Use the book band colour your child is reading in school to help you make a good choice. *Rabbit and Crab* is a good choice for children reading at Orange Band in their classroom to read independently.

The aim of independent reading is to read this book with ease, so that your child enjoys the story and relates it to their own experiences.

About the book

Rabbit and Crab grow and harvest carrots together. Rabbit tries to be crafty and suggests a race to decide who gets all the carrots. Crab is clever and finds a way to beat Rabbit in the race.

Before reading

Help your child to learn how to make good choices by asking:
"Why did you choose this book? Why do you think you will enjoy it?"
Look at the cover together and ask: "What do you think the story will be about?" Ask your child to think of what they already know about the story context. Then ask your child to read the title aloud.
Ask: "What do you think Rabbit and Crab are doing? What do you know about what rabbits usually eat?"
Remind your child that they can sound out the letters to make a word if they get stuck.
Decide together whether your child will read the story independently or read it aloud to you.

During reading

Remind your child of what they know and what they can do independently. If reading aloud, support your child if they hesitate or ask for help by telling the word. If reading to themselves, remind your child that they can come and ask for your help if stuck.

After reading

Support comprehension by asking your child to tell you about the story. Use the story order puzzle to encourage your child to retell the story in the right sequence, in their own words. The correct sequence can be found at the bottom of the next page.

Help your child think about the messages in the book that go beyond the story and ask: "Why did Rabbit suggest having a race? Do you think it was a fair suggestion?"

Give your child a chance to respond to the story: "Did you have a favourite part? Did you think Rabbit would win the race? Why/why not?"

Extending learning

Help your child understand the story structure by using the same story pattern and adding different elements. "Let's make up a new story about an animal that tries to play a trick on another animal. Which animals are in your story? What task could they be sharing? How might one of them try to trick the other?"

In the classroom, your child's teacher may be teaching about punctuation such as te use of exclamation marks. There are several examples in this book that you could look at with your child, for example: *Ready, steady, go! / You tricked me!*
Find these together and try reading out loud with expression.

Franklin Watts
First published in Great Britain in 2022
by Hodder and Stoughton

Copyright © Hodder and Stoughton Ltd, 2022

Series Editors: Jackie Hamley and Melanie Palmer
Series Advisors: Dr Sue Bodman and Glen Franklin
Series Designers: Peter Scoulding and Cathryn Gilbert

A CIP catalogue record for this book is
available from the British Library.

ISBN 978 1 4451 8399 2 (hbk)
ISBN 978 1 4451 8400 5 (pbk)
ISBN 978 1 4451 8459 3 (library ebook)
ISBN 978 1 4451 8460 9 (ebook)

Printed in China

Franklin Watts
An imprint of
Hachette Children's Group
Part of Hodder and Stoughton
Carmelite House
50 Victoria Embankment
London EC4Y 0DZ

An Hachette UK Company
www.hachette.co.uk

www.reading-champion.co.uk

Answer to Story order: 4, 5, 2, 1, 3